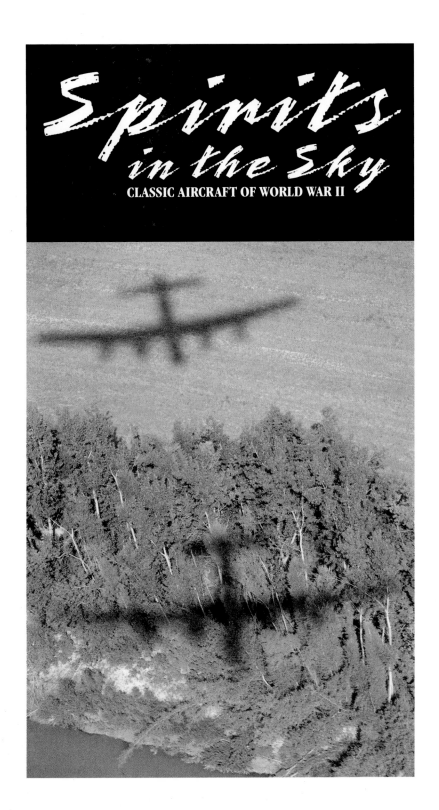

Spirits
in the Sky
CLASSIC AIRCRAFT OF WORLD WAR II

Spirits in the Sky

in the Sky

CLASSIC AIRCRAFT OF WORLD WAR II

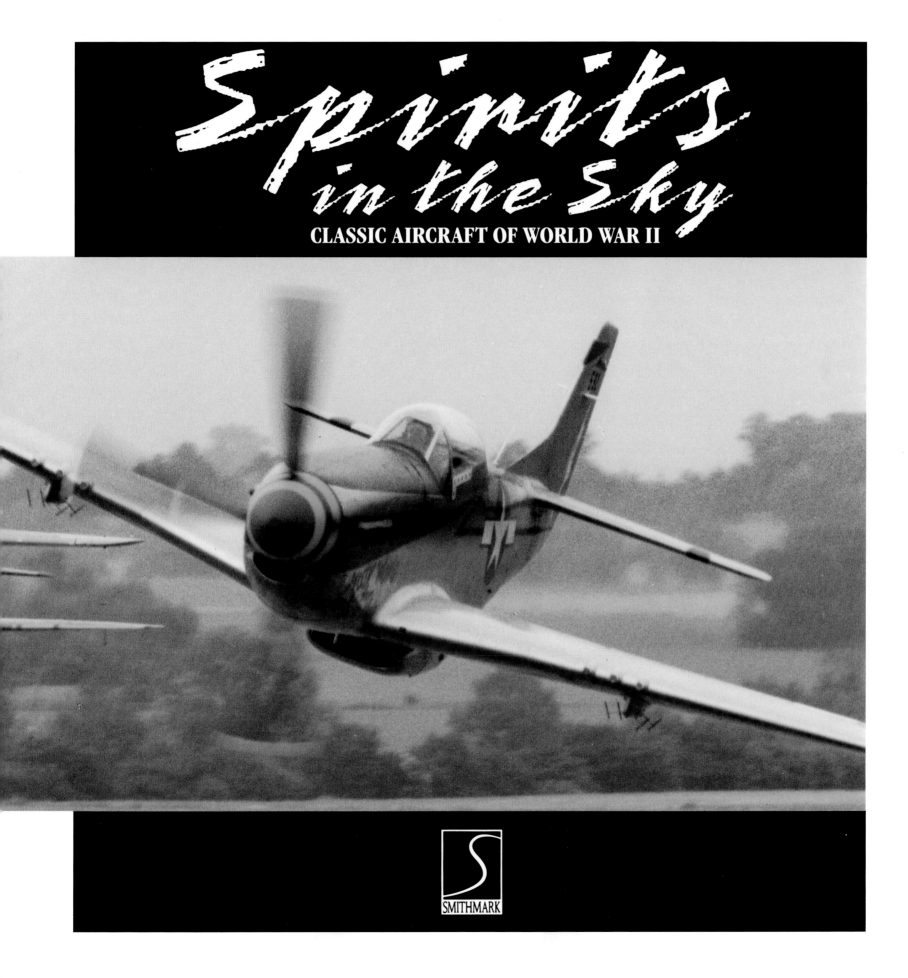

SMITHMARK

A Salamander Book

© Salamander Books Ltd 1992.
129-137 York Way,
London N7 9LG,
United Kingdom

ISBN 0-8317-6824-X

0 9 8 7

This edition first published in the United States in 1992 by SMITHMARK Publishers Inc., 16 East 32nd Street New York, NY 10016

SMITHMARK books are available for bulk purchase for sales promotion and premium use. For details write or telephone the Manager of Special Sales, SMITHMARK Publishers Inc., 16 East 32nd Street New York, NY 10016 (212) 532-6600

All correspondence concerning the content of this volume should be addressed to Salamander Books Ltd.

Editor: Chris Westhorp
Designers: Paul Johnson, Louise Bruce and John Heritage
Color artwork: © Pilot Press Ltd, England
Filmset by The Old Mill, London

Color Reproduction by P & W Graphics PTE Ltd, Singapore

Printed and bound in China

Credits
Every effort has been made to trace the holders of copyright material quoted and that which appears does so courtesy of the respective copyright holders, where known. The sources are: **Jacket, front flap**: interview with James Goodson in *Antenna*, magazine of RAF Chicksands, 19 September 1986. **Page 12**, *Avenger at War* by Barrett Tillman, Ian Allan, Shepperton 1979. **Page 16**, "Kamikaze Song of the Warrior", source unknown. **Page 20**, *Aerial Combat Escapades* by J. Hunter Reinburg, GCBA Publishing, Arizona 1988. **Page 26**, "I Saw Regensburg Destroyed" by Beirne Lay Jr in the *Saturday Evening Post*, Washington 1943. **Page 40**, *Nine Lives* by Group Captain Alan Deere DSO, OBE, DFC, Hodder & Stoughton, London 1958; **Page 42**, author interview with Ernst Schröder. **Page 44**, *Back Every Friday* by Air Marshal Peter Wykeham KCB, DSO, OBE, DFC, AFC. **Page 48**, author interview with Roland Baker. **Page 52**, *Hell Divers: US Navy Dive-Bombers at War* by John F. Forsyth, Motorbooks International, Wisconsin 1991. **Page 56**, *Fighter Pilot* by Wing Commander Paul Richey DFC, Leo Cooper, London 1950. **Page 60**, *The Bedford Triangle* by Martin W. Bowman, Patrick Stephens Ltd, Somerset 1988. **Page 64**, *Enemy Coast Ahead* by Wing Commander Guy Gibson VC, DSO, DFC, Michael Joseph Ltd, London 1946. **Page 78**, *Xavier* by Richard Heslop, Hart-Davis MacGibbon, London 1970. **Page 82**, "Return to Florence" by First Lieutenant Benjamin C. McCartney, USAAF, in *National Geographic*, Washington, March 1945. **Page 86**, *The Last Enemy* by Richard Hillary, Macmillan London Ltd., 1942. **Page 98**, *Mission Completed* by Air Chief Marshal Sir Basil Embry GCB, KBE, DSO, DFC, AFC, Landsborough Publications. **Page 102**, author correspondence with Captain Peter Hardiman. **Page 122**, *The Face of Victory* by Group Captain Leonard Cheshire VC, Hutchinson & Co, London 1961; **Page 128**, author correspondence with Captain Peter Hardiman. **Page 134**, *Way of a Fighter* by Major General Claire Lee Chennault, Putnam, New York 1949. **Page 142**, *Fighter Pilot* edited by Stanley M. Ulanoff, Prentice Hall, New York.

Photo Credits
The publishers would like to thank the following individuals and organizations for their assistance in producing this book: Air Vice Marshal John Alison; Bob Anderson; Squadron Leaders Colin Paterson, Chris Stevens and Andy Tomalin, and Group Captain Cliff Spink OBE of The Battle of Britain Memorial Flight; Tony Craig and Peter Henley of British Aerospace PLC; Flight Lieutenant Charlie Brown; Derek Bunce; The Champlin Fighter Museum, Mesa, Arizona; Bill Bryan, Bill Clark, Joe Coleman, Bob and Bobby Collings, Jason and Ric Harmon, Craig McBurney, Rusty Restuccia, John Rising and Gary Young of The Collings Foundation; Mary Collins; Russ Anderson and Herschel Whittington of The Confederate Air Force; Susan D'Arcy and David Puttnam of Enigma Films Ltd; Chris Edmondson and Peter Jarvis of EAA Aviation; Paul Bonhomme, Nick and Stephen Grey, and Hoof Proudfoot of The Fighter Collection; Arthur Gibson; Frank Crosby, David Henchie and Carole Stearn of the Imperial War Museum, Duxford; Paul Morgan; John Pitchforth of Nikon UK; Mark and Ray Hanna of The Old Flying Machine Company; Charles Pereira; Rolf Meum, Lars Ness and Anders Saether of The Scandinavian Historic Flight; and Dale Donovan and Mike Hill of Strike Command Public Relations.

All the colour photographs in this book were taken by Patrick Bunce on Kodachrome film from Kodak UK, using Nikon cameras and lenses supplied by Nikon UK.

Endpapers: P-47 Thunderbolt
Page 1: Lancaster
2/3: Left to right, P-40 Kittyhawk, Spitfire, P-51 Mustang
4/5: B-17 Flying Fortress
6: B-17 bombsight
7: B-24 Liberator (top), A6M Zero (below)
8: Bf 109G
9: F6F Hellcat
10: P-51 Mustang (top); B-29, B-17 and B-24 (bottom)
11: B-24

Contents

Introduction

On 17 August 1942 a force of 12 B-17 Flying Fortress bombers of the 8th Air Force, based in East Anglia and led by Major Paul Tibbetts, headed for Rouen, France, in the first American heavy bomber raid on occupied Europe in World War II. It was a small beginning and their bomb loads were not great. Tibbetts' bombardier on this inaugural raid was Tom Ferebee. Three years later, to the month, the same bombardier was aboard Tibbetts' "Enola Gay", a Boeing B-29 Superfortress based at Tinian in the Marianas, when it released the first Atomic bomb to be dropped in warfare onto the Japanese city of Hiroshima.

More that 45 years later the same scene is re-enacted annually by the Confederate Air Force's "Fifi', the only airworthy B-29 in the world. Aircraft such as this are a living testament to the great air battles of World War II. Today, the Battle of Britain, Pearl Harbor and the great carrier battles in the Pacific unfold dramatically at air shows around the world. They are watched by a generation who were not even born when the first Mustangs and Spitfires, Lancasters and Liberators, took to the skies.

In 1940 the German "Blitzkrieg" quickly overwhelmed Holland, Belgium and France and by the summer of 1940 the Wehrmacht was poised to cross the English Channel. All that stood between Britain's survival and a total German victory were a few hundred RAF and Empire pilots, volunteers from North America, and airmen from the occupied nations of Europe, ably supported by thousands of men and women in defence installations, aircraft and munitions' factories. They achieved the impossible. Sleek Supermarine Spitfires, gutsy Hawker Hurricanes and a few Gloster Gladiator biplanes, all scraped together in the United Kingdom's hour of greatest need, stood like the thin red line in the Crimea. Together, they defeated the massed formations of Messerschmitt Bf 109s, 110s, Heinkels and Dorniers.

America's fragile neutrality was finally broken by the surprise Japanese attack on the US Navy base at Pearl Harbor, on the Hawaiian island of Oahu, in the early morning of Sunday 7 December 1941. Formations of Mitsubishi Zero fighters and Nakajima Kate torpedo bombers reached Oahu, split into elements and roared over the island at low-level, machine gunning P-40 Warhawks and PBY Catalinas at Wheeler Field and Kanaohe. Bombers pounded Hickam Field. Torpedo bombers and Aichi Val dive bombers flew over Battleship Row at Pearl Harbor. The USS *Arizona* exploded in a pall of smoke and flame and within about 25 minutes seven other battleships had either been destroyed or were damaged and listing.

The "Tora, Tora, Tora" scenario, which re-enacts the Japanese attack on Pearl Harbor, is probably the centrepiece at the Confederate Air Force (CAF) show. One real Zero is joined by AT-6 Texans, painted in the colours of the Imperial Japanese Air Force Zeros, and Vultee Valiant aircraft, modifed and painted to represent Kate torpedo bombers. They take off in droves, formate and dive as spectacular explosions roar skywards. The pilots, some wearing Japanese headbands, simulate dogfights with Grumman Wildcats and P-40 Warhawks while bombers criss-cross at various heights. Where else too would one see five B-25s re-enact the famous 18 April 1942 "Doolittle Raid" on Tokyo, or Grumman Wildcats and Hellcats duelling with Japanese Zeros in a re-creation of the great Pacific battles of 1942-45?

The colourful spectacle presented by restored fighters and bombers can often dim the memory of the intense air fighting fought out in all theatres of war. Few people give much thought to the problems of freezing high-altitude weather conditions and jammed machine guns, a feathered propeller or a shattered tail fin, when pristine warbirds are paraded in all their splendour. Can it really be a Westland Lysander and a P-40 Kittyhawk in the air? It seems incredible that aircraft such as these have survived to delight new generations of enthusiasts. Much of this is due to restoration groups who spend thousands of hours repairing worn out airframes and scouring the land for a missing machine gun, Plexiglas turret or tail wheel.

Warbirds usually take pride of place at air shows, whether it be Abbotsford in Canada, Duxford, Cambridge-shire (home of The Old Flying Machine Company and The Fighter Collection), or The Shuttleworth Collection at tranquil Old Warden in the heart of Bedfordshire, England. The Shuttleworth Collection is the proud owner of several restored veterans, among them a Gloster Gladiator and a Supermarine Spitfire. Visitors to its air shows include the de Havilland Mosquito, nicknamed the "Wooden Wonder" because of its construction. Props and pistons reign supreme at these cradles of aviation. In America a loving public watch with unbridled passion as Mustangs, Bear-cats and others, are raced around the circuit at Reno. At Whittman Field, Oshkosh, in the farming State of Wisconsin, the annual EAA (Experimental Aircraft Association) fly-in is the largest aerial spectacular in the world; literally thousands of aircraft fly in to the convention each year, including a large contingent of warbirds. One of the most famous is the recently restored Collings Foundation B-24J

Liberator "All American". In 1943, Liberators from bases in North Africa painted desert pink carried out a near-suicidal, low-level strike on the Ploesti oilfields in Romania. In 1990, when "All American" won Grand Champion at EAA Oshkosh and EAA Lakeland, modern successors were applying similar pink war paint for combat in the Gulf.

The camouflage patterns of fighters such as the F4U Corsair and Bf 109 look immaculate sitting at dispersal. It is only when the mighty engines start their throaty roar and propeller blades are whipped into action that one is aware of the immense power these majestic machines produce. Kicking up clouds of dust and grass in their wake, a Martin Marauder and an Avenger taxi out, their multi-bladed propellers scything through the air like medieval swordsmen. This is what people come to see. History on the move, formations in the air; a colourful procession both varied and seemingly never-ending.

There is no finer aerial sight than a B-24 flying formation with a B-17 and a Lancaster. This unique flight has been performed at the National Warplane Museum's air show which takes place at Geneseo in New York State each year. Geneseo's B-17G "Fuddy Duddy" and the Canadian Warplane Heritage's Lancaster, based just across the border at Hamilton, Ontario, take off by bumping along the grass strip with all the grace of an ungainly Canada goose, before soaring aloft to join Dave Tallichet's B-24 "Delectable Doris". Down below, multi-coloured striped canvas marquees, with their streamers fluttering from the centre poles,

are dotted around like medieval jousting tents. Two P-51D Mustangs clad in chromium, silver and blue, roar past like shining knights on chargers.

The show over, there are sightseeing flights and queues for steak suppers. Larry Goldstein, a former 8th Air Force radio-operator, looks at his fellow diner's steak and says, jokingly, "Eat it, you could be in Stalag Luft III this time tomorrow!" A local band plays and older members, dance, unabashed, forties' style. Catalinas and Forts taxi by, blowing the canvas mess tent with their prop-wash in scenes reminiscent of "M*A*S*H" and take-off time in "Catch 22". The most incongruous sight must be Yankees and Confederates eating at the same tables, but these are Yankee Air Force and Confederate Air Force members though, not "Bluebellies" and "Rebs"!

In France the Jean Salis Collection's annual La Ferte Alais air show takes place on a grass plateau near the village of Cerney. Take away the spectators and it would not be difficult to imagine one had wandered onto the set of "The Blue Max". A Swedish Fieseler Storch and a Merlin-engined CASA 1112, painted a mottled green-grey to represent Bf 109 camouflage, provide an international flavour. The mighty-engined F8F Bearcat and UK contingent of Spitfire and Hurricane, B-25 Mitchell and a P-47 Thunderbolt from Duxford, draw large, admiring crowds. In World War II, P-47s were nicknamed "Jugs" (short for the Hindu god "Juggernaut") because to fly the beast was considered suicidal. Gallic pride is prominently to the fore with the

collection's own F4U-5NL Corsair and two P-51D Mustangs, "Jumping Jacques" and "Empire of the Sun" — the latter used in the movie of the same name.

While it is a most enjoyable experience to view warbirds from the ground, the ultimate experience is to photograph them from the air. B-17G "Sentimental Journey", which belongs to the Arizona Wing of the CAF, is an excellent mount. Take-off is extremely smooth and a sound like a kettle coming to the boil confirms that the tail wheel is seeking the recess immediately behind the Cheyenne tail turret. B-25 Mitchell "Devil Dog" is out in front, to port is "Texas Raiders" and behind there are two P-51s flying top cover. The formation tightens up and the enormous Boeing wing and huge Wright Cyclones blot out the shape of "Texas Raiders" as "Sentimental Journey" pulls in close, its Hamilton props whirling away only a few inches from the Plexiglas nose. Wartime commanders extolled the virtues of close formation flying to improve survival over enemy territory. Their ghostly ancestors must be brimming with pride in the heavens above as the B-17's wingtip snuggles up to the "Raiders" waist. "Devil Dog" maintains

its position in the van while the two P-51s in trail dart and weave from side to side like playful outriders.

The formation turns and alarming puffs of cloud appear; not Flak but large belts of white cumulus. "Sentimental Journey" breaks formation at around 2,500ft (760m), leaving the other heavies and their "little friends" to return to base. The hard working pilots are perspiring heavily. It is in sharp contrast to the 8th Air Force bomber crews flying from wartime England when freezing conditions at altitude were unbearable. A radio operator who dropped an orange was amazed to see it smash like cut glass on contact with the radio room floor.

Ready for landing! Back through the narrow cockpit hatch, along the precarious narrow catwalk over the bomb bay, where two dummy 500 pounders hang suspended, to the waist. It is all extremely difficult. In heavy flight gear it must have been well nigh impossible. In a swirling, negative G spiral with engines out it was almost certain death for the majority of crews.

"Sentimental Journey", however, completes her mission. No acrid smoke from her machine guns and no expended shells littering the floor of the waist section. A landing so smooth one could stand upright as she skims the tarmac. Large crowds, waving and cheering on the flight line, are reminiscent of the homecoming in the 1943 version of "Memphis Belle", 30 missions and then Stateside!

Obtaining air-to-air photographs, like the ones featured in this book, can sometimes be hazardous. During the remake of "Memphis Belle" shooting had only just begun when "Lucky Lady", a French-owned B-17, lost its No.1 engine. The number five cylinder seized and blew completely off. The cowling furled back like a peeled banana, falling in fields below, but not before it had taken a chunk out of the B-17's tailplane. Stephen Grey, pilot of an accompanying Mustang, did exceptionally well to avoid the debris. "Lucky Lady" returned to Duxford safely on three engines. Worse followed when filming moved to RAF Binbrook. On 25 July 1989, a second French B-17 crashed on take-off and all 10 passengers and crew had a narrow escape when it was destroyed in the ensuing fire.

During World War II scenes like this were not uncommon on the numerous airfields used by the 8th and 9th Air Forces that dotted the English countryside. Living conditions were described as "rugged" so, in an effort to brighten their surroundings, GI artwork, in the form of vivid murals, cartoons and buxom girls, appeared on the walls of Nissen huts, briefing rooms and messes.

Fifty years later some examples can still be found, but many more have disappeared. Fortunately, an ever increasing band of enthusiasts ensure that the same fate will not befall the magnificent warbirds that were born in war and restored in peace. Long may they flourish.

TBF/TBM Avenger

"We dived down over the left side of the screen and broke through the AA fire, approaching the torpedo release point at 240kts at 400ft. The convoy opened fire but it was too late."

Larry French was among those who flew one of war's classic torpedo strike aircraft — the Grumman Avenger — which emerged from a shattering debut at the Battle of Midway to reign supreme in the Pacific. It also served valiantly aboard carriers in the treacherous North Atlantic and saw widespread action with the Royal Navy and the US Marines until final victory.

A preserved Avenger gathers momentum as it thunders past during a warbirds display. The American "arsenal of democracy" enabled the Allies to gear up production of new torpedo bombers for the Pacific and Atlantic theatres to avenge the "day of infamy" which saw Pearl Harbor blasted and ravaged.

Engine cowls open like gills on large killer sharks, two
Avengers shudder and shake as their Wright Cyclone radials
are run at full power. Six TBF-1s were the first to see action in
May 1942 during the plucky defence of Midway Island. They
launched a suicidal attack on the Japanese invasion fleet and
all except one of the torpedo bombers were destroyed.

Origin: Grumman Aircraft Engineering Corporation.
Type: Three-seat torpedo bomber.
Engine: One 1,700hp Wright R-2600-8 or -20 Cyclone 14-cylinder two-row radial.
Dimensions: Span 54ft 2in (16.5m); length 40ft (12.2m); height 16ft 5in (5m); wing area 490ft² (45.52m²).
Weights: Empty (TBF-1) 10,100lb (4,580kg); (TBM-3) 10,545lb (4,787kg), loaded (TBF-1) 15,905lb (7,214kg); (TBM-3) 18,250lb (8,278kg); (TBM-3E) 17,895lb (8,117kg).
Performance: Maximum speed (TBF-1) 278mph (445km/h); (TBM-3) 267mph (430km/h); initial climb (TBF-1) 1,075ft (376m)/min; service ceiling (TBF, TBM-1 to -3) about 23,400ft (7,132m); (TBM-3E) 30,100ft (9,175m); range with full weapon load, 1,010-1,215 miles (1,600-1,950km).
Armament: (TBF-1, TBM-1) one 0.30in Browning in upper forward fuselage, one 0.5in in dorsal power turret and one 0.30in manually aimed in rear ventral position; internal bay for one 22in torpedo or 2,000lb (907kg) of bombs; TBF-1C, TBM-1C, TBM-3 added one 0.5in in each outer wing and underwing racks for eight 60lb (27kg) rockets.

Illustrated below: (from top to bottom): This TBF-1 of VT-8 from USS *Hornet* was the only survivor of a group of six from the Avenger's first combat mission; a Mk II, one of 400 serving with the Royal Navy, note the D-Day markings.

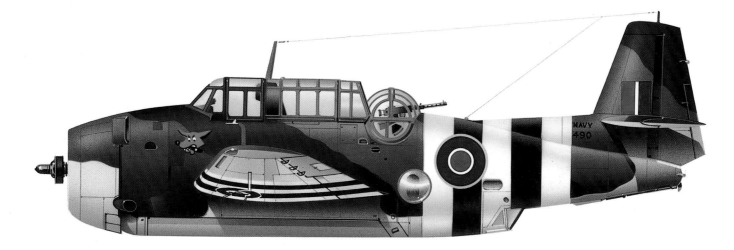

F8F Bearcat

"In serving on the seas, be a corpse saturated with water; in serving on land be a corpse covered with weeds; in serving in the sky, be a corpse that challenges the clouds."

Grumman's Hellcat replacement was designed to stifle the "Kamikaze Song of the Warrior" (quoted above) by destroying the suicide planes which threatened the Pacific fleets converging on Japan, but the sun was to set on the sons of the seven Samurai before the stocky navy fighter could unleash its full fury in the enemy's lair.

The sun glints on the highly polished starboard wing of the diminutive Bearcat as it soars away into the "wild blue yonder", hanging on the four props attached to its powerful Pratt & Whitney radial. The Bearcat forged a link between the great World War II fighters and the early jets, many of which it outperformed in Indo-China.

"Oh, I have slipped the surly bonds of Earth. And danced the
skies on laughter-silvered wings: Sunward I've climbed and
joined the tumbling mirth. Of sun-split clouds — and done a
hundred things."
John Gillespie MacGee's famous poem "High Flight" aptly
describes this scene of a Bearcat soaring majestically in the heavens.

Despite some 880 design changes during development,
which delayed its entry into first-line service, the ''Big-Tailed
Beast'' never looked back after entering combat in the
campaign for Rabaul in late 1943. It delivered bombs and
depth charges with high-level accuracy and strafed enemy
targets with cannon, rocket and machine gun fire.

Origin: Curtiss-Wright Corporation.
Type: Two-seat carrier-based dive bomber; data for SB2C-1.
Engine: 1,700hp Wright R-2600-8 Cyclone 14-cylinder two-row radial.
Dimensions: Span 49ft 9in (15.2m); length 36ft 8in (11.2m); height 16ft 11in (5.1m); wing area 422ft² (39.20m²).
Weights: Empty 11,000lb (4,990kg); loaded 16,607lb (7,550kg).
Performance: Maximum speed 281mph (452km/h); service ceiling 24,700ft (7,530m); range 1,110 miles (1,786km).
Armament: Two 20mm of four 0.50in guns in wings and two 0.30in or one 0.50in in rear cockpit; provision for 1,000lb (454kg) bombload internally (later versions added wing racks).

Illustrated below: (from top to bottom): SB2C-3 of VB-3 aboard USS *Hancock* in a three-tone finish; a glossy, sea blue SB2C-3 from VB-80, also aboard USS *Hancock*.

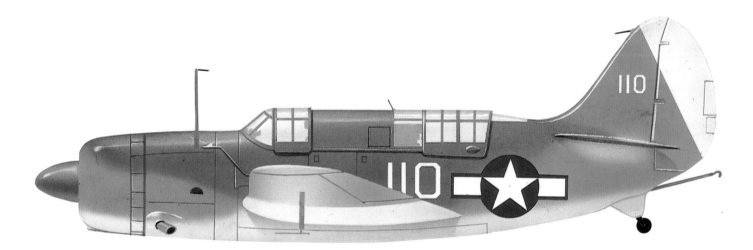

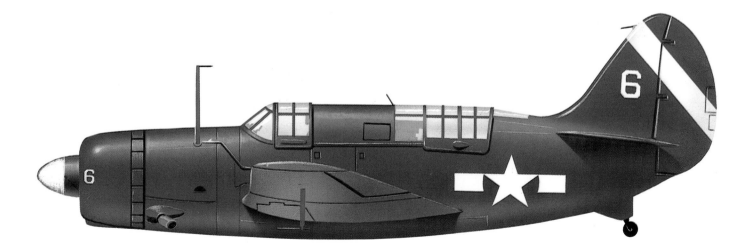

Hurricane

" 'Line astern-Go!' came Johnny's quiet voice over the radio. We watched Johnny go down, his little Hurricane looking graceful but deadly on to the still-diving Hun."

Paul Richey was one of the heroic "Johnnies" in the thin blue line in the blazing summer of 1940 when Goering's massed air fleets pounded the defenders' sceptred isle. Highly-manoeuvrable with a rock solid platform for its eight Brownings, this thoroughly warlike machine was the mount for the majority of "The Few".

The Fighter Collection's rare, Canadian-built Hurricane XIIB, based at the old Battle of Britain airfield at Duxford, wears the colours of No 71 (Eagle) Squadron, RAF, as a tribute to the American pilots who volunteered to fight for Britain before the USA entered the war. It is the world's only privately-owned aerobatic Hurricane.

"Scramble!" Hurricane XIIB, sporting its famous "fighting eagle" insignia, buzzes Duxford in a "beat up" routine which recalls the days of the famous Duxford Wing when Bader's "Bus Company" cut wave after wave of murderous German assaults to rags and tatters and thus created a day — 15 September — now celebrated as Battle of Britain Day.

Origin: Hawker Aircraft Ltd.
Type: Single-seat fighter; later, fighter-bomber and tank-buster.
Engine: One Rolls-Royce Merlin vee-12 liquid-cooled.
Dimensions: Span 40ft (12.19m); length 32ft (9.75m); (Mk I) 31ft 5in; height 13ft 1in (4m).
Weights: Empty (I) 4,670lb (2,118kg); (IIA) 5,150lb (2,335kg); (IIC) 5,640lb (2,558kg); (IID) 5,800lb (2,631kg); (IV) 5,550lb (2,515kg); loaded (I) 6,600lb (2,994kg); (IIA) 8,050lb (3,650kg); (IC) 8,250lb (3,742kg); (IID) 8,200lb (3,719kg); (IV) 8,450lb (3,832kg).
Performance: Maximum speed (I) 318mph (511km/h); (IIA, B, C) 345mph (560km/h); (IID) 286mph (460km/h); (IV) 330mph (531km/h); initial climb (I) 2,520ft (770m)/min; (IIA) 3,150ft (960m)/min; (rest, typical) 2,700ft (825m)/min; service ceiling (I) 36,000ft (10,973m); (IIA) 41,000ft (12,500m); (rest typical) 34,000ft (10,365m); range (all, typical) 460 miles (740km).
Armament: (I) eight 0.303in Brownings; (IIA) same, with provision for 12 guns and two 250lb bombs; (IIB) 12 Brownings and two 250 or 500lb bombs; (IIC) four 20mm Hispano cannon and bombs; (IID) two 40mm Vickers S guns and two 0.303in Brownings; (IV) universal wing with two Brownings and two Vickers S, two 500lb bombs, eight rockets, smoke installation or other stores.

Illustrated below: (from top to bottom): Gloster-built Mk I in No 73 Sqn markings; Hurricane IID of No 6 Sqn in the Western Desert, July 1942.

A-26 Invader

"We avoided the balloons. Radar was unable to pick up our blip although we had a little gunfire. Slowing our air speed we dropped the agents in the correct field."

Whether it was dropping OSS "Joes" on the outskirts of Berlin one dark, rainy night in 1945 — as told by Lieutenant Bill Miskho, a visual navigator aboard a gloss black A-26C — or skipping low over the Normandy hedgerows before and after D-Day, the speedy twin-engined firebrand was more than a match for German defences.

Beautiful head-on shot of an A-26B on take-off shows, to terrific effect, the substantial nose mounted armament of eight 0.50in calibre machine gun and a 20mm cannon which packed a mighty wallop. The Invader served for a quarter of a century, Algeria, before its squadron swansong flying night interdiction missions over Vietnam.

Framed by two red-lipped radials, Varga's "Heavenly Body" shows the flag as she wings through the sky, pointing the way like a figure-head on a ship for the crowded flight deck of "Sugarland Express". Ed Heinemann's imperious design was the last propeller-driven, twin-engined bomber to be produced for the US Air Force.

Origin: Douglas Aircraft Company.
Type: Three-seat attack bomber; FA-26 reconnaissance, JD (Navy) target tug.
Engines: Two 2,000hp Pratt & Whitney R-2800-27, -71 or -79 Double Wasp 18-cylinder two-row radials; on post-war Mark B-26K, 2,500hp R-2800-103W.
Dimensions: Span 70ft (21.43m) (B-26K, 75ft, 22.86m, over tip tanks); length 50ft (15.24m); height 18ft 6in (5.64m); wing area 540ft² (50.17m²).
Weights: Empty, typically 22,370lb (10,145kg); loaded, originally 27,000lb (12,247kg) with 32,000lb (14,515kg) maximum overload, later increased to 35,000lb (15,876kg) with 38,500lb (17,460kg) maximum overload.
Performance: Maximum speed 355mph (571km/h); initial climb 2,000ft (610m)/min; service ceiling 22,100ft (6,736m); range with maximum bombload 1,400 miles (2,253km).
Armament: (A-26B) ten 0.50in Brownings, six fixed in nose and two each in dorsal and ventral turrets; internal bombload of 4,000lb (1,814kg), later supplemented by underwing load of up to 2,000lb (907kg); (A-26C) similar but only two 0.50in in nose; (B-26K, A-26A) various nose configurations with up to eight 0.50in or four 20mm, plus six 0.30in guns in wings and total ordnance load of 8,000lb (3,628kg) in bomb bay and on eight outerwing pylons.

Illustrated below: (from top to bottom):
A-26B "Stinky" of 552nd Bomb Sqn, 386th Bomb Group, 9th Air Force, in April 1945; B-26C supplied to France for use in Algeria in the 1950s.

Lancaster

"The city of Lincoln was silent . . . I suppose it was a wonderful sight, these great, powerful Lancasters in formation, off on a journey. We were off to the dams."

Wing Commander Guy Gibson, who wrote these words, and the legendary Lanc' are justifiably famous for the RAF's most daring and audacious low-level attack."Enemy Coast Ahead!" was the chilling cry that prefaced many a trip to the Ruhr as the nocturnal bombers fought to rip out the heart of the Reich and reap the whirlwind.

Four Merlins purr in unison as "City of Lincoln" crosses the Lincolnshire wolds en route to a rendezvous with its BBMF stablemates. Built in 1945 for service in the Far East, the RAF's only remaining flyable Lanc', out of 7,377 built, was intended for Tiger Force until atomic bombs forced Japan's total surrender.

There can be no finer sight to fire the imagination than to
witness a Lancaster thundering low overhead, Merlins straining
at the leash. One can almost hear the anxious cry ''Corkscrew!''
in this magnificent tail gunner's eye-view of the Canadian
Warplane Heritage's B. Mk X in a scene which is similar to 1944
when No. 6 Group RCAF set out for Berlin.

Canadians operating from ''bomber counties'' in north-east
England carried the war to Germany in squadrons named
''Bison'', ''Thunderbird'' and ''Moose''. Appropriately, the
CWH Lanc' is clad in colours to represent the aircraft in
which Andrew Mynarski was killed over France in 1944
when his valiant sacrifice earned a posthumous VC.

Silhouetted against the sky like a scene from "Target for Tonight", "City of Lincoln" heads serenely home to Coningsby. Roy Chadwick's supremely successful design was immortalized by RAF and Dominion crews whose nightly timetable was to rain bombs on German cities in a frightening, Wagnerian apocalypse until the ultimate, inevitable, Armageddon.

Origin: A. V. Roe Ltd; also Armstrong Whitworth, Vickers-Armstrongs, UK, and Victory Aircraft, Canada.
Type: Seven-seat heavy bomber.
Engines: Four 1,460hp Rolls-Royce or Packard Merlin 20 or 22 (Mk II only: four 1,650hp Bristol Hercules VI, 14 cylinder two-row, sleeve-valve radials).
Dimensions: Span 102ft (31.1m); length 69ft 4in (21.1m); height 19ft 7in (5.97m).
Weights: Empty 36,900lb (16,705kg); loaded 68,000lb (30,800kg).
Performance: Maximum speed 287mph (462km/h) at 11,500ft (3500m); cruising speed 210mph (338km/h); service ceiling 24,500ft (7467m); range with 14,000lb (6350kg) bombs: 1,660 miles (2675km).
Armament: Nose and dorsal turrets (Mk II also ventral) with two 0.303in Brownings (some, including Mk VII, had Martin dorsal turret with two 0.50in), tail turret with four 0.303in Brownings, bomb bay carrying normal load of 14,000lb (6350kg) or 22,000lb (9979kg) bomb if modified.

Illustrated below: (from top to bottom): Lancaster B.III of No 617 Sqn in May 1943, specially modified for the 'Upkeep' dam-busting mine; Lancaster B.I (Special) of No 617 Sqn in 1945 armed with the 'Grand Slam' bomb; Lancaster B.I of No 419 Sqn in 1945, its yellow fin boss denoting it is the G-H radar-equipped flight leader.

Origin: Glenn L. Martin Co.

Type: Five- to seven-seat medium bomber.

Engines: Two Pratt & Whitney Double Wasp 18-cylinder two-row radials; (B-26) 1,850hp R-2800-5; (A) 2,000hp R-2800-39; (B, C, D, E, F, G) 2,000hp R-2800-43.

Dimensions: Span (B-26, A and first 641 B-26B) 65ft (19.8m); (remainder) 71ft (21.64m); length (B-26) 56ft (17m), (A, B) 58ft 3in (17.7m); (F, G) 56ft 6in (17.23m); height (up to E) 19ft 10in (6.04m); (remainder) 21ft 6in (6.55m); wing area (65ft) 602ft² (55.93²), (71ft) 658ft² (61.13m²).

Weights: Empty (early, typical) 23,000lb (10,433kg); (F, G) 25,300lb (11,490kg); maximum loaded (B-26) 32,000lb (14,515kg); (A) 33,022lb (14,980kg); (F) 38,000lb (17,235kg); (G) 38,200lb (17,340kg).

Performance: Maximum speed (up to E, typical) 310mph (500km/h); (F, G) 280mph (451km/h); service ceiling (up to E) 23,000ft (7,000m); (F, G) 19,800ft (6,040m); range with 3,000lb (1,361kg) bomb load (typical) 1,150 miles (1,850km).

Armament: (B to E) one 0.50in manually aimed in nose, twin-gun turret, two manually aimed 0.50in waist guns, one "tunnel gun" (usually 0.50in), two 0.50in in power tail turret and four 0.50in fixed as "package guns" on sides of forward fuselage; (F, G) same but without tunnel gun. Internal bomb load of 5,200lb (2,359kg) up to 641st B, after which rear bay was disused (eliminated in F, G) to give maximum load of 4,000lb (1,814kg).

Illustrated below: (from top to bottom): B-26B-55 of 397th Bomb Group at Dreux, France, in September 1944; Marauder IA of No 14 Sqn, RAF, at Fayid, Egypt, in late 1942 operating in the torpedo-bombing role.

Messerschmitt Bf 109

"Fighter pilot's emotions are those of the duellist — cool, precise, impersonal. He is privileged to kill well. If one must kill or be killed, it should be done with dignity."

Richard Hillary, who penned these words in the *The Last Enemy,* faced his anonymous adversaries in their cold, clinical Bf 109s over England in 1940. Willy Messerschmitt's nimble but rugged fighting machine won its spurs in Spain and then duelled to the death over Mother Russia, the Western Desert and, finally, the Fatherland itself.

A welcome addition to the sound of the Merlin in modern air show dogfights is the noise of an original fuel-injected Daimler Benz powerplant in this Bf 109G "Gustav" which saw service with JG 77 in Libya. A favourite mount of many Luftwaffe aces, today the "Augsburg Eagle" is a much sought after warbird, but only a handful now exist out of 34,000.

In the air and on the ground the menacing '109 is
remembered as the famous arch-foe of the Spitfire and
Hurricane. This perfectly restored "Gustav" was built at
Leipzig in 1942 and saw brief service with JG 77 in Libya
before being captured and sent to Britain for RAF evaluation.
In 1991 it flew again for the first time since 1945.

At Duxford, The Old Flying Machine Company's ''Bf 109J'',
painted in the markings of Jagdgeschwader 26 based in
France and Malta, shows off its clipped lines in a power pass.
Really a Buchon, it was originally built for the Spanish Air
Force in 1943. The star of many films, it was powered by a
Hispano-Suiza engine before the installation of a Merlin.

"Achtung Spitfire!" During 1943-44 Bf 109s flown by crack
fighter units like the "Battling Bastards of Brunswick" and
the "Abbeville Kids" were feared by Allied fighter and
bomber crews, but now the MOD's Bf 109 is at peace in the
air alongside former combatants like the Spitfire, with whom
many friendly duels are fought in the skies over Duxford.

Origin: Bayerische Flugzeugwerke.
Type: Single-seat fighter (many, fighter bomber).
Engine: (B, C) one 635hp Junkers Jumo 210D inverted-vee-12; (D) 1,000hp Daimler-Benz DB 600Aa; (E) 1,100hp DB 601A, 1,200hp DB 601N or 1,300hp DB 601E; (F) DB 601E; (G) 1,475hp DB 605A-1, or other sub-type up to DB 605D rated 1,800hp.
Dimensions: Span (A to E) 32ft 4½ in (9.87m); (others) 32ft 6½ in (9.92m); length (B, C) 27ft 11in; (D, E, typical) 28ft 4in (8.64m); (F) 29ft 0½ in; (G) 29ft 8in (9.04m); height (E) 7ft 5½ in (2.28m); (others) 8ft 6in (2.59m).
Weights: Maximum loaded (B-1) 4,850lb; (E) 5,523lb (2,505kg) to 5,875lb (2,665kg); (F-3) 6,054lb; (G) usually 7,496lb (3,400kg).
Performance: Maximum speed (D) 323mph; (E) 348-354mph (560-570km/h); (G) 353-428mph (569-690km/h); range on internal fuel (all) 365-460 miles (typically, 700km).
Armament: Highly varied, principal-build G-6 had one 30mm MK 108, two MG 131 above engine and two MG 151 under wings.

Illustrated below: (from top to bottom): Bf 109D of Jagdfliegershule 1, 1940; Bf 109E-7B of II Gruppe, near Stalingrad in 1942; Bf 109G-6 of IV/JG5 in winter snow-speckled camouflage.

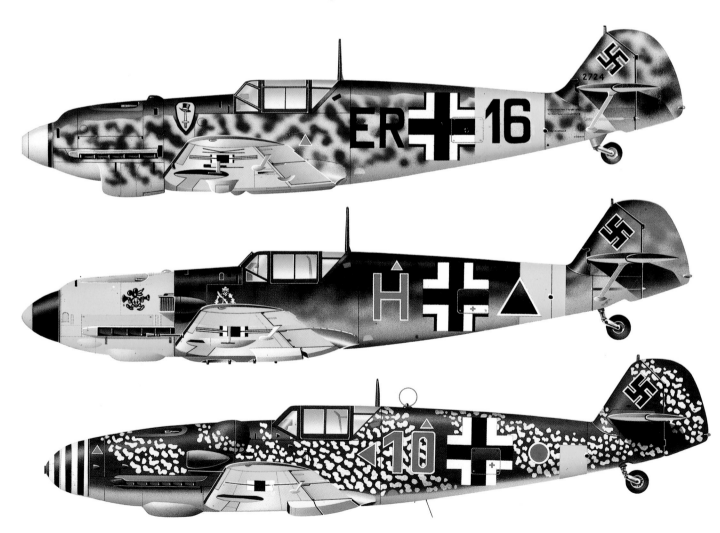

B-25 Mitchell

"When Jimmy's plane buzzed down the Hornet's *deck there wasn't a man who didn't help sweat him into the air. One pilot hung on the brink of a stall until we nearly catalogued his effects. . ."*

Thus wrote Admiral "Bull" Halsey, who watched Jimmy Doolittle lead his celebrated Tokyo raiders off the heaving deck of the USS *Hornet*. Named for General Billy Mitchell, these dependable destroyers masthead-bombed in the Pacific, pounded positions in northern Italy and blasted Panzer columns in Normandy.

A silver-skinned Mitchell in pristine condition at dispersal, machine guns at the ready. Devastating firepower was a feature of the twin-tailed bomber, whether it was the hard-hitting machine guns that strafed Japanese aircraft at Rabaul, or an omnipotent 75mm cannon which blasted ships and ground targets in the lagoons and atolls of the Pacific.

Bomb bays open against a smoke filled sky or touching down at Geneseo Valley, "Panchito" rekindles visions of strikes in the Pacific where the type wreaked havoc among Japanese shipping with novel skip-bombing tactics and strafing runs with nose-mounted 75mm cannon. In July 1945 a B-25 made headlines when it hit the Empire State Building in New York.

"Panchito" banks low over North American skies to reveal the concentrated firepower that was a feature of the type. Rotating turrets and bristling machine guns were more than a match for any enterprising Zero or '109 pilot trying to add to his score. When employed in the ground attack role B-25s could train 14 0.50in calibre machine guns on the target.

North American's large, yet agile medium bomber, which was designed as a light, fast attacker, has never been better illustrated than in this climbing shot of ''Yankee'' pulling gently into the blue. Adaptable and reliable, B-25s performed a multiplicity of roles for the Free Dutch and French and the US, RAF and Russian air forces too.

Origin: North American Aviation Inc.
Type: Medium bomber and attack, with crew of four to six.
Engines: (B-25, A, B) two 1,700hp Wright R-2600-9 Cyclone 14-cylinder two-row radials; (C, D, G) two 1,700hp R-2600-13; (H, J, F-10); two 1,850hp R-2600-29.
Dimensions: Span 67ft 7in (20.6m); length (B-25, A) 54ft 1in (16.7m); (B, C, J) 52ft 11in (16.1m); (G, H) 51ft (15.54m); height 15ft 9in (4.80m); wing area 610ft² (56.67m²).
Weights: Empty (J, typical) 21,100lb (9,580kg); maximum loaded (A) 27,100lb (12,293kg); (B) 28,640lb (12,991kg); (C) 34,000lb (15,422kg); (G) 35,000lb (15,876kg); (H) 36,047lb (16,350kg); (J) overload 41,800lb (18,960kg).
Performance: Maximum speed 275mph (443km/h); service ceiling (late models, typical) 24,000ft (7,315m); range (all, typical) 1,500 miles (2,414m).
Armament: (J) 13 0.50in guns plus a bomb load of 4,000lb (1,814kg); an attack version of the J was fitted with a solid nose carrying five extra 0.50in guns.

Illustrated below: (from top to bottom): B-25C-15 of 488th Bomb Sqn in Tunisia, 1943; B-25J-32 of 499th Bomb Sqn "Bats Outa Hell", Ie Shima, July 1945; B-25J of 498th Bomb Sqn "Falcons", Luzon, Philippines, 1945.

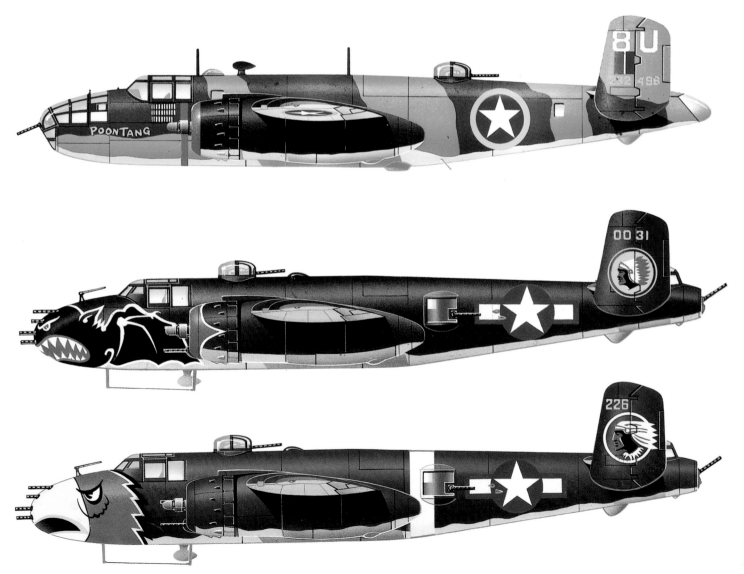

Mosquito

"I pulled up over the Shell House, then down almost to street level. I could see flak bursting just above the roof tops. A Mosquito passed over us, not more than ten feet above."

De Havilland's remarkable, radical design caused alarm among its enemies by day and by night. Basil Embry's words describe the daring, low-level strike on a Gestapo HQ in The Netherlands; one of many pin-point, morale-boosting raids made by the "Wooden Wonder" to help free the subjugated peoples of Europe from Nazi tyranny.

This close-up view shows the remarkable Mosquito over the patchwork quilt of England and evokes memories of "633 Squadron", a film which offered a whole new generation of aviation enthusiasts the chance to re-run, in flashback, the time when enemy sirens wailed in nervous anticipation of the "Mossie's" unwelcome approach.

Built of wood to economise on scarce metals "Mossies" were
assembled by a variety of wartime cottage industries, like this
T. Mk III which was one of 50 built at the London Omnibus
Co in Leavesden in 1945. Now owned by Hawker Siddeley
Aviation, it retains the fictional "HT-E" codes applied by
make-up artists during the filming of "633 Squadron".

Origin: The de Havilland Aircraft Company.
Type: Designed as high-speed day bomber, but many subsequent variants were developed.
Engines: (Mks II, III, IV and early VI) two 1,230hp Rolls-Royce Merlin 21 or (late FB.VI) 1,635hp Merlin 25. Other variants received uprated Merlins.
Dimensions: Span 54ft 2in (16.5m); length (most common) 40ft 6in (12.34m); height (most common) 15ft 3½ in (4.66m).
Weights: Empty (Mks II-VI) about 14,100lb (6,396kg); maximum gross (Mks IV and VI) about 22,500lb (10,200kg).
Performance: Maximum speed, 380mph (612km/h) for III, IV and VI, 410mph (660km/h) for IX, XVI and 30; service ceiling, 34,500ft (10,520m) for most marks, up to 44,000ft (13,410m) for the Mk XV; combat range, typically 1,860 miles (2,990km).
Armament: Four 20mm cannon under the floor and four 0.30in machine guns in the nose fitted in most models; (B.IV) four 500lb (227kg) bombs carried internally; (FB. VI) two 250lb (113kg) bombs in rear bay and two on wing racks or eight 60lb (27kg) rockets; (B. IX) bulged bay for 4,000lb (1,814kg) bomb; (FB.XVIII) one 57mm Molins gun and eight 60lb (27kg) rockets; (Mk.33) torpedo capability.

Illustrated below: (from top to bottom): PR. XVI of US 8th Air Force's 653rd Bomb Sqn (Light) at Watton, Norfolk; B. XVI of No. 371 Sqn, Oakington, in late 1944.

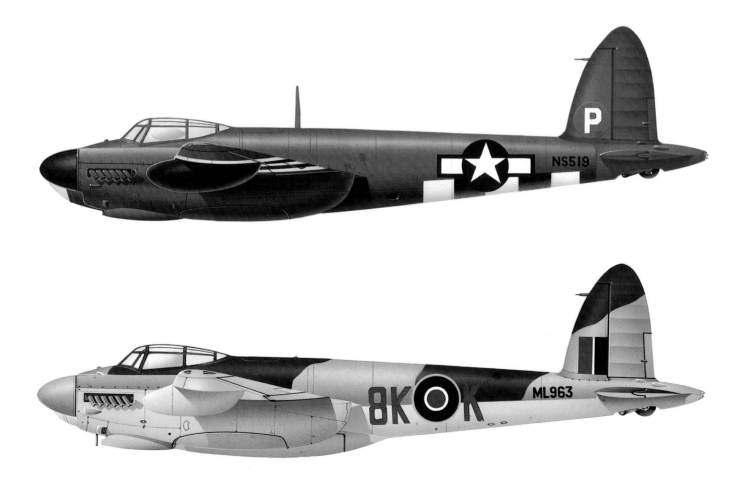

P-51 Mustang

"Compared to any fighter I had seen or flown she was beautiful. I fell in love at first sight. Finally, North American Aviation had kept their word and given us the best fighter ever designed."

Pete Hardiman, an 8th Air Force P-51 pilot, sums up the finest fighter of World War II which escorted the "heavies" to their German targets and back again. Like silver bullets in a Germanic legend, these shiny, aluminium-skinned "little friends" helped deliver the coup-de-grâce to the German werewolf in its Berchtesgarten lair.

A sight to start the pulse racing — two Mustangs in a low-level "beat up" after returning from an imaginary fighter sweep over France or train-busting in Germany. Whatever the reason, connoisseurs the world over love to see these magnificent chargers galloping unrestrained across the sky, their throaty Merlins purring in shared admiration.

Yellow swastikas and a squadron emblem are mirrored in the highly-polished port wing of ''Petie 3rd'', which is painted in the colours of its famous forebear, ''Petie 2nd'', which Lieutenant Colonel John C. Meyer of the 487th Fighter Squadron, 352nd Fighter Group, flew in England from August 1944 to January 1945, notching up 23 aerial victories.

Incongruously perhaps, The Old Flying Machine Company's
P-51D was painted "Ding Hao!" (Chinese for "very good")
when it appeared in the film "Memphis Belle", but then this
Australian licence-built Mustang was re-built in Hong Kong in
the mid-1970s. "Double Trouble Two" wears the famous yellow
and black chequer colours of the 353rd Fighter Group.

Black painted blades whirl in frantic rotation while silver side panels hide a powerful Packard Merlin behind a shimmering fusion of light and grace. ''Hurry Home Honey'' wears the colours of Major Richard A. Peterson of the 364th Fighter Squadron, 357th Fighter Group, who racked up 15½ aerial kills in two P-51s of the same name in 1944-45.

Flaps down, David Gilmour taxies his red-nosed "Debden Eagle" home after a sortie aloft. In World War II the famed 4th Fighter Group was composed of former "Eagle Squadron" pilots like Gentile and Blakeslee — American volunteers who had flown and fought for Britain in her hour of greatest need before joining the 8th Air Force.

When long-range P-51 Mustangs began appearing over Berlin,
and even escorting the ''heavies'' on shuttle missions to
Russia, Hermann Goering knew his fighters could not halt the
Allies' round-the-clock assault on German towns and cities.
Combat crews in the big bombers were loud in their praise of
the èlan of the P-51 pilots who watched over them.

On occasion, single-seat fighters landed and made a timely
pick-up of downed airmen and flew them safely home before
they became prisoners of the Third Reich. This P-51
wears the wartime colours of ''Old Crow'', flown by Captain
Clarence E. Anderson of the 363rd Fighter Squadron, 357th
Fighter Group, who destroyed 16¼ enemy aircraft in 116 missions.

Ground pounders kept the P-51s flying in all climates despite battle damage and the constant threat of enemy action. So successful were they that by 1945 Mustangs were knocking on the doors of Berlin and Tokyo in ever increasing numbers. Undoubtedly the finest fighter of the war, the P-51 fought in North Africa, Italy, France and the Pacific.

Origin: North American Aviation Inc.
Type: (P-51) single-seat fighter; (A-36) attack bomber.
Engine: (P-51, A-36) one 1,150hp Allison V-1710-F3R, later (P-51D) 1,590hp V-1650-7 (Packard licence-built R-R Merlin).
Dimensions: Span 37ft 0½in (11.29m); length 32ft 2½in (9.81m); height 13ft 8in (4.1m); wing area 233ft² (21.65²).
Weights: Empty (P-51D) 7,125lb (3,230kg); maximum loaded (P-51D) 11,600lb (5,260kg).
Performance: Maximum speed (P-51D) 437mph (703km/h); initial climb (early) 2,600ft (792m)/min, (P-51D) 3,475ft (1,060m)/min; service ceiling (P-51D) 41,900ft (12,770m); range with maximum fuel (P-51D) 1,300 miles (2,092km) with drop tanks.
Armament: P-51 four 20mm Hispano cannon in wings; (A-36A) two 0.50in in cowling and four in wings, and wing racks for two 500lb (227kg) bombs; (all subsequent P-51 production models) six 0.50in Browning MG53-2 with 270 or 400 rounds each, and wing racks for tanks or two 1,000lb (454kg) bombs; (Cavalier or Turbo, typical) six 0.50in with 2,000 rounds, two hardpoints each 1,000lb, and four more each 750lb.

Illustrated below: (from top to bottom): A-36A of the 27th Fighter-Bomber Group, Corsica, in July 1944; note the 190 mission symbols. Mustang III of the RAF's No 19 Sqn in the summer of 1944.

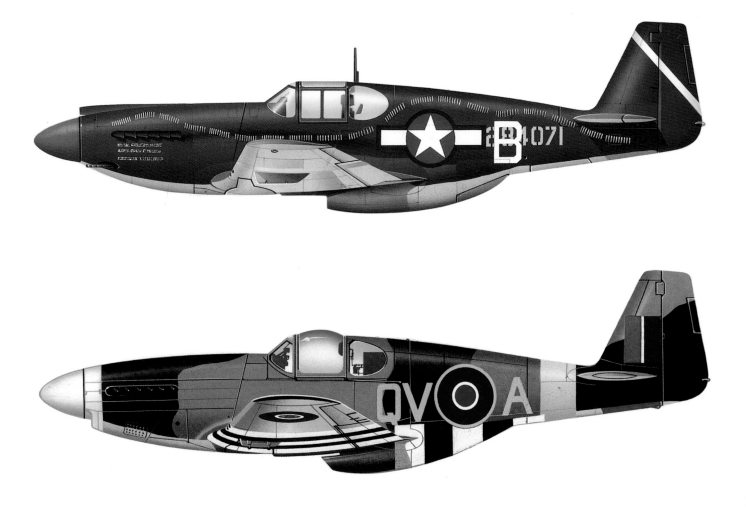

Spitfire

"The little Spitfire somehow captured the imagination of the British people at a time of near despair, becoming a symbol of defiance and of victory in what seemed a desperate and almost hopeless situation."

Thus spoke the test pilot Jeffrey Quill. More than a supremely successful fighter, the Spitfire was indeed the material symbol of final victory to the British and the envy of the Luftwaffe. A ballerina-like aeroplane with immense aesthetic appeal, it was the distillation of years of experience with Schneider Trophy seaplanes, aircraft that endowed it with a distinguished pedigree.

"Fire over England!" seems an appropriate cry as the legendary fighter from the Supermarine studio gracefully banks into the sunlit cloud in a pageant of aerial mastery and magnificence. This seemingly delicate, yet robust, little machine still takes centre stage at all the world's air shows and plays to the galleries just as Bader, Lacy and Tuck did.

During the Battle of Britain ground crews worked through the night at airfields such as this, the pilots arriving before dawn to prepare for the day's combat. The air was filled with the cacophony of Merlin engines being tested. Later, the order to scramble sent pilots sprinting for their aircraft, and engines once again roared into life, this time for real.

The now legendary Rolls-Royce Merlin and Griffon engines were vital to the success of the Spitfire. Shoe-horned into its compartment forward of the cockpit without a square inch to spare, it was the heart of the machine. Its combination with the unmistakeable lines of the Spitfire frame was the perfect marriage between irresistible raw power and sturdy elegance.

Like crossed swords the immortal Spitfire and Hurricane duel
playfully above the peaceful English countryside over which
Dowding's young men staved off wave after wave of German
bombers in 1940. Two years before, Duxford had become the
Spitfire's first home, the type marking a quantum leap in
aircraft design when it replaced the Gauntlet biplanes.

"Never in the field of human conflict was so much owed...to so few", wrote Winston Churchill upon the victorious conclusion of the Battle of Britain. Two Spitfires belonging to The Old Flying Machine Company show off their elliptical wings as they perform aerobatics over Cambridgeshire in a re-enactment of the battle for a new generation of admirers.

This tantalising triumvirate of Spits in tight formation could
almost be a fighter sweep over the continent in late 1944 as
evidenced by the ''invasion'' stripes and a multi-national
flavour provided by Ray Hanna's Mk IX in the roundels of the
Belgian Air Force. And no marriage would be complete
without a Rolls Royce — the Griffon-powered Mk XIV.

Inquisitive Spitfire XIX and Hurricane of the Battle of Britain
Memorial Flight tail-chase their Lancaster mother ship
en route to Fairford. Five Spitfires are operated by the RAF but
this Hurricane, ironically in the markings of James Nicholson
VC who was badly burned in 1940, caught fire and
crashed in September 1991.

"Ring this bell and run like hell" announced the call to "scramble" as "The Few" leapt aboard their waiting Spitfires, charged into the fray and battled with enemy raiders high in the sky over southern England. This ex-Indian Air Force T. Mk VII was bought by Stephen Grey in 1980 and restored to a single-seat LF. Mk IXe at Booker in 1984.

Origin: Supermarine Aviation Works (Vickers) Ltd.
Type: Single-seat fighter, fighter-bomber or reconnaissance.
Engine: One Rolls-Royce Merlin or Griffon vee-12.
Dimensions: Span 36ft 10in (11.23m), clipped, 32ft 2in; length 29ft 11in (9.12m), later, with Griffon engine, typically 32ft 8in (9.96m); height 11ft 5in (3.48m), with Griffon, typically 12ft 9in (3.89m).
Weights: Empty (Mk I) 4,810lb (2,182kg). (IX) 5,610lb (2,545kg); (XIV) 6,700lb (3,040kg); maximum loaded (I) 5,784lb (2,624kg); (IX) 9,500lb (4,310kg); (XIV) 10,280lb (4,663kg).
Performance: Maximum speed (I) 362mph (580km/h); (IX) 408mph (657km/h); (XIV) 448mph (721km/h); initial climb (I) 2,530ft (770m)/min; (IX) 4,100ft (1,250m)/min; (XIV) 4,580ft (1,396m)/min; range on internal fuel (I) 395 miles (637km); (IX) 434 miles (700km); (XIV) 460 miles (740km).
Armament: (Mk I, Mk XIII) four 0.30in machine guns; (Mk IA, IIA, VA) eight 0.30in; (Mk IB, IIB, VB Mk VI, Mk F.XIV) two 20mm cannon and four 0.30in; (Mk VC) choice of guns plus two 250lb (113kg) bombs; Mk Vs all fitted with centreline rack for 500lb (227kg) bomb; (Mk IXE, Mk F.XIVE) two 20mm cannon and two 0.50in machine guns; (Mk 21) four 20mm cannon and 1,000lb (454kg) bombs.

Illustrated below: (from top to bottom): PR. XI of USAF's 7th Photo Group in 1944, Mk VB of the Forca Aerea Portuguesa in 1943.

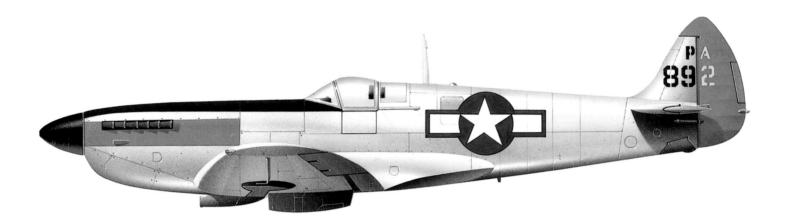

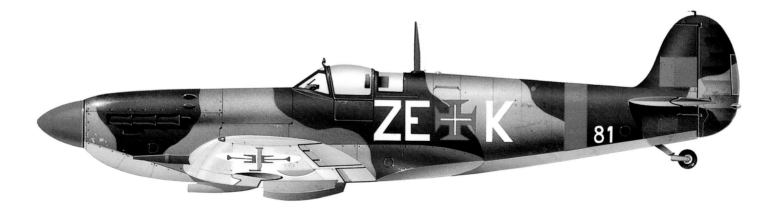

B-29 Superfortress

"Fifty miles away to starboard, the bomb went off. How pale by comparison Wilhelmshaven; how insignificant Bergerac. Yes, and with such utter devastation before our very eyes."

Somewhat prophetically, in 1942 a B-17 bombardier sang "I Don't Want to Set The World on Fire" over his intercom. This was three years before Boeing's big brother systematically fire-stormed Japanese cities and then reduced two of them to ashes in the dawn of a nuclear age. Leonard Cheshire observed one of the atomic drops, at Nagasaki, in August 1945.

A fierce sunrise over Texas and a B-29 Superfortress at repose conjures up a vision of the atomic flash which signalled the end of World War II. Boeing's massive machine dwarfed its little brother, the B-17, and would have replaced it had Germany not surrendered earlier. Post-war, B-29s equipped SAC and RAF Bomber Command in anticipation of new conflict.

"Fifi" is a magnificent sight as the huge bomber casts a giant shadow coming into land at Rebel Field, home of the Confederate Air Force. From the start, the Boeing pedigree was evident in the sleek design whose high-aspect wing, pressurized cabins and 10-gun armament in remotely controlled power turrets, placed it far ahead of its contemporaries.

"Fifi" shows off its four powerful supercharged Wright R-3350s which can develop 2,200 hp at sea-level. Although it had not flown for 17 years, when the USAF allowed the CAF to select a B-29 near China Lake, California, this chilling omen of global warfare was restored to flying condition and flown triumphantly to Harlingen, Texas, in 1971.

Its 3,000mile (5,080km) range with 12,000 pounds (5,443kg) of bombs dictated that the B-29 equip units in the Pacific. In India in the spring of 1944, the dreaded "Bni-Ju's", as the Japanese came to call them, flew the Himalayas, moving in supplies to forward bases in China, before commencing high-level bombing and low-level fire-raids on Japan.

Origin: Boeing Airplane Co.
Type: High-altitude heavy bomber, with crew of 10-14.
Engines: Four 2,200hp Wright R-3350-23 Duplex Cyclone
18-cylinder radials each with two turbochargers.
Dimensions: Span 141ft 3in (43.05m); length 99ft (30.2m);
height 29ft 7in (9.02m); wing area 1,739ft² (161.56m²).
Weights: Empty 74,500lb (33,795kg); loaded 135,000lb (61,240kg).
Performance: Maximum speed 357mph (575km/h) at
30,000ft (9,144m); cruising speed 290mph (467km/h);
service ceiling 31,850ft (9,708m); range with 10,000lb
(4,540kg) bombs 3,250 miles (5,230km).
Armament: Four GE twin-0.50in turrets above and below,
sighted from nose or three waist stations; ball tail turret,
with own gunner, with one 20mm cannon and twin 0.50in
or three 0.50in; internal bombload up to 20,000lb (9,072kg).
Carried first two nuclear bombs.

Illustrated below: (from top to bottom):
B-29-45-BW of 500th Bomb Group, 73rd Bomb Wing in the
Pacific, 1945; RB-29A-45-BN operating on strategic reconnaissance
duties; B-29 based on Tinian in 1945 and carrying
Bombing Through Overcast (BTO) radar.

127

P-47 Thunderbolt

"To taxi took an act of Congress. Taking off was a kick in the pants! Brute energy in action. Climbed like a homesick angel. Heads for the deck like a rock."

Pete Hardiman describes Republic's famous "Thunder-jug", a gigantic chariot flown by saddle-sore pilots on long escort missions in a roller-coaster ride to paradise, or to hell and back. In the ETO and over the jungles of Burma, enemies sacrificed themselves in the path of its deadly, destructive firepower.

Darkening skies over Duxford form an appropriate backdrop to one of the most powerfully built thoroughbreds to see fighter combat in World War II. The chequerboard cowling and "No Guts — No Glory!" inscription complete the livery of Lieutenant Ben Mayo's 78th Fighter Group "T-bolt" which was based at the Cambridgeshire station in 1944.

"No Guts — No Glory!" is propelled into the air by brute force supplied by an 18 cylinder radial, with all the finesse of a giant hand grabbing the rear of the beast and thrusting the monster machine heavenwards. Once airborne, the "Jug" was totally destructive but some, like the 56th Fighter Group, jealously preferred it to the more nimble P-51.

Beautifully sculptured lines extol the virtues of the bubble-top canopy which sits like a long teardrop on the fuselage of ''Big Ass Bird II''. T-bolts, and especially P-47F ''razorback'' models, are very rare but in recent years the arrival of six P-47Ms from Peru has improved the spectacle of these large gunslingers on the world's air show circuits.

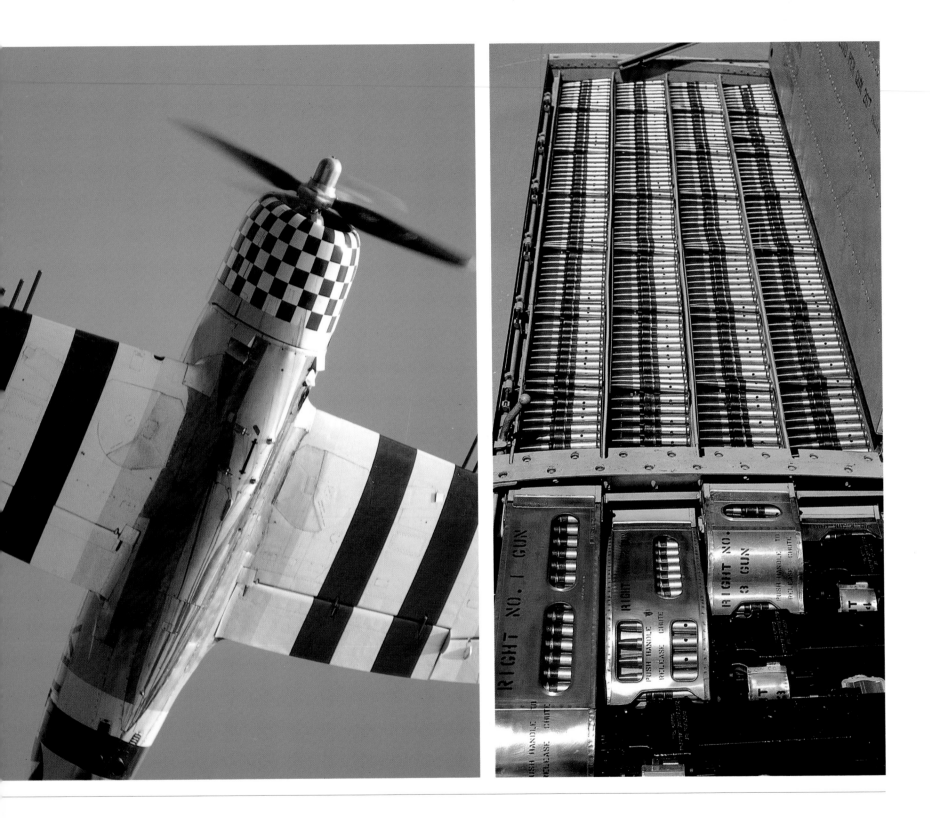

Republic's recalcitrant bronco was a weighty beast, made heavier by eight 0.50in calibre guns with over 2,000 rounds. She proved almost impossible to reign in, so it took guts to dive several thousand feet and pull her out before the ''Jug'' sacrificed its pilot. This P-47M has a Peruvian ancestory and a hot-blooded latin temperament to match.

Origin: Republic Aviation Corporation.

Type: Single-seat fighter; (D and N) fighter-bomber.

Engine: One Pratt & Whitney R-2800 Double Wasp 18 cylinder two row radial; (B) 2,000hp R-2800-21; (C, most D) 2,300hp R-2800-59; (M, N) 2,800hp R-2800-57 or -77.

Dimensions: Span (except N) 40ft 9¼ in (12.4m), (N) 42ft 7in (12.98m); length (B) 34ft 10in (10.6m); (C, D, M, N) 36ft 1¼ in (11.03m); height (B) 12ft 8in (3.8m); (C, D) 14ft 2in (4.3m); (M, N) 14ft 8in (4.5m); wing area (exceptN) 300ft² (27.87m²), (N) 322ft² (29.9m²).

Weights: Empty (B) 9,010lb (4,087kg); (D) 10,700lb (4,853kg); maximum loaded (B) 12,700lb (5,760kg); (C) 14,925lb (6,770kg); (D) 19,400lb (8,800kg); (M) 14,700lb; (N) 21,200lb (9,616kg).

Performance: Maximum speed (B) 412mph; (C) 433mph; (D) 428mph (690km/h); (M) 470mph; (N) 467mph (751km/h); initial climb (typical) 2,800ft (855m)/min; service ceiling (B) 38,000ft; (C-N) 42,000-43,000ft (12,800-13,000m); range on internal fuel (B) 575 miles (952km); (D) 1,000 miles (1,600km); ultimate range (drop tanks) (N) 2,350 miles (3,800km).

Armament: (Except M) eight 0.50in Colt-Browning M-2 in wings, each with 267, 350 or 425 rounds; (M) six 0.50in; (D and N) three to five racks for external load of tanks, bombs or rockets to maximum of 2,500lb (1,134kg).

Illustrated below: (from top to bottom): P-47D-30 of 9th Air Force's 366th Fighter Sqn was active against retreating German forces in 1944; P-47D-30-RA serving with 512th Fighter Sqn in northern occupied Germany, 1945.

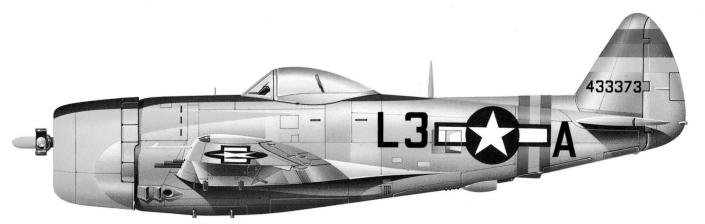

P-40 Warhawk

"When the Americans saw the Buffaloes drop like flies under the Japanese onslaught over Rangoon, P-40 stock rose until finally AVG pilots refused to trade Hurricanes for P-40s."

Claire Chennault, CO of the "Flying Tigers". Never a match for the dogfighting Zero at altitude, these shark-toothed devils, flown by wily "Yank" volunteers, still held their own in China. A pre-war design, Warhawks saw action on all fronts while RAF Kittyhawks fought admirably in the Western Desert.

A P-40 resplendent in Chinese Nationalist markings heads for the deck after pulling out of a dive. Although vastly inferior to the Zero, American Volunteer Group pilots, using hit and run tactics, destroyed 286 Japanese aircraft by capitalizing on the ruggedness, weight and superior diving qualities of this remarkable fighter.

All that is missing in this bloodthirsty line up of sharks teeth and a skull's vacant stare, are a pair of crossbones. Many wartime artists used cowlings for canvas and those in the ''Flying Tigers'' copied designs from the *India Illustrated Weekly* which depicted RAF shark-nosed P-40s in the desert. Chennault's fearsome fighters proved equally effective.

Americans called them Warhawks but the RAF, possibly along more traditional lines, aptly named the stalwart fighters first Tomahawk and then Kittyhawk. This P-40N Kittyhawk, which is owned by The Fighter Collection, was assigned to the RCAF in 1943 and wears the colours of No 122 "Shark Mouth" Squadron in the Western Desert.

A setting sun throws this long nosed fighter into sharp relief
but the outline, characterised by its cowl length intake and
bulbous radiator housing, is unmistakably that of a Warhawk
on the prowl. Despite the Allison engine's poor high-altitude
performance, the P-40 acquitted itself well, serving with no
less than 28 Allied air forces on all fronts.

Curtiss' uncomplicated, yet remarkably effective design is
justifiably famous for its exploits with the AVG in China.
Despite being outclassed by its more illustrious
contemporaries, it emerged with reputation intact,
seeing fierce fighting on the Russian Front and becoming
the RAF's most important fighter in the Mediterranean.

Not a favourite among those who flew her, the P-40
nevertheless proved a reliable workhorse. While vilified for
its lack of agility, it was lauded for its delightful handling
characteristics and sturdiness. The distinctive sharksmouth
markings lent a fiercer aspect than perhaps deserved yet
survive today as a powerful and familiar evocation of the war.

Origin: Curtiss-Wright Corporation.

Type: (A) single-seat fighter, (B) single-seat fighter, reconnaissance and ground attack; (C, D) single-seat fighter bomber.

Engine: (A) P-36A, 1,050hp Pratt & Whitney R-1830-13 Twin Wasp 14-cylinder two-row radial; Hawk 75A and Mohawk, 1,200hp Wright GR-1820-G205A Cyclone nine-cylinder radial; (B) 1,040hp Allison V-1710-33 vee-12 liquid-cooled.

Dimensions: Span 37ft 3½in (11.36m); length (A) 28ft 7in (8.7m), (B) 31ft 8½in (9.7m), (C) 31ft 2in (9.55m) or 33ft 4in (10.14m); (D) 33ft 4in (10.14m); height (A) 9ft 6in (2.89m), (B, C, D) 12ft 4in (3.75m).

Weights: Empty (A) 4,541lb (2,060kg), (B) 5,812lb (2,636kg), (C) 6,550lb (2,974kg), (D) 6,700lb (3,039kg); loaded (A) 6,662lb (3,020kg), (B) 7,459lb (3,393kg), (C) 8,720lb (3,960kg).

Performance: Maximum speed (A) 303mph (488km/h), (B, D) 345mph (555km/h), (C) 364mph (582km/h); initial climb (A) 2,500ft (762m)/min, (B) 2,650ft (807m)/min, (D) 2,120ft (646m)/min.

Armament: (A) P-36A, one 0.50in and one 0.30in Brownings above engine; P-36C, as P-36A with two 0.30in in wings.

Illustrated below: (from top to bottom): Tomahawk IIB (AK401) of the RAF in 1941 with four "kills" credited; P-40 of 55th Sqn, 20th Pursuit Group, Marsh Field, California, 1941; Tomahawk IIB of 154 IAP, Red Banner Baltic Fleet Air Force, Leningrad, 1942.

F4F/FM Wildcat

"O'Hare made his attack runs with perfect flight form His shooting was wonderful — absolutely deadly. I saw three blazing Japanese falling — he shot them down so quickly."

John Thach "Butch" O'Hare's wingman wrote this the day he downed five Japanese bombers in a single action. Outclassed by the Zero, Grumman's fighting cat nevertheless earned a well deserved reputation for rugged dependability, and in the hands of skilled pilots it emerged victorious in many gunfights in Europe and the Pacific.

This revealing underbelly shot of the stubby Wildcat shows off its sturdy and economical shape to an admiring audience. Initially, the Wildcat was designed as a biplane but it emerged a magnificent monoplane fleet fighter, holding the Japanese at bay in the Pacific and then being relegated to the smaller escort carriers with the arrival of the Hellcat.

Origin: Grumman Aircraft Engineering Corporation.
Type: Single-seat naval fighter.
Engine: (XF4F-2) one 1,050hp Pratt & Whitney R-1830-66
Twin Wasp 14-cylinder two-row radial; (F4F-3) 1,200hp
R-1830-76; (F4F-4 and FM-1) R-1830-86; (FM-2) 1,350hp
R-1820-56.
Dimensions: Span 38ft (11.6m); length 28ft 10in, (8.5m);
height 11ft 11in (3.6m); wing area 260ft² (24.15m²).
Weights: Empty (F4F-3) 4,425lb, (F4F-4) 4,649lb, (FM-2)
4,900lb (2,226kg); loaded (F4F-3) 5,876lb, (F4F-4) 6,100lb
(2,767kg), rising to 7,952lb (3,607kg) with final FM-1s;
(FM-2) 7,412lb (3,362kg).
Performance: Maximum speed (F4F-3) 325mph (523km/h),
(F4F-4, FM-1) 318mph (509km/h), (FM-2) 332mph
(534km/h); initial climb, typically 2,000ft (610m)/min;
service ceiling, typically 35,000ft (10,670m) (more in light
early versions); range, typically 900 miles (1,448km).
Armament: (XF4F-2) two 0.50in Colt-Brownings in
fuselage; (F4F-3) four 0.50in in outer wings; (F4F-4 and
subsequent) six 0.50in in outer wings; (F4F-4, FM-1 and
FM-2) underwing racks for two 250lb (113kg) bombs.

Illustrated below: (from top to bottom): F4F-3 of VF-7
aboard USS *Wasp* in December 1940; FM-1 in semi-gloss
sea blue from USS *Block Island*, 1944.

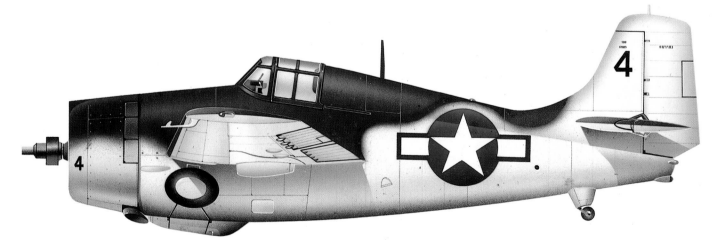